With gratitude to the many children who shared their feelings about divorce to help create this book, it is dedicated to my stepson, Bill, who was 10 when his parents divorced.

ADDITIONAL COPIES: For individual
copies send $6.95 plus applicable tax and
$2.50 to cover the cost of handling to
WOODLAND PRESS.
QUANTITY DISCOUNT RATES are
available for hospitals, schools, churches
and others who need more than 12 copies.
Write for details.

WOODLAND PRESS
99 WOODLAND CIRCLE
MINNEAPOLIS, MN 55424
(612) 926-2665

A FACILITATOR GUIDE is available for
$20.00 and includes additional information
for leading a structured children's grief
support group.
FACILITATOR TRAINING WORKSHOPS
are offered in Minneapolis, MN. Contact
Woodland Press for more information.

PRINTED IN THE U.S.A.

ABOUT THIS BOOK

This book was created to help children ages 6-12 learn about divorce and the feelings of grief. Divorce creates stressful feelings of grief from loss and change. Children who are unable to understand or verbally express their feelings often act them out in unhealthy ways.

The art process allows children to express symbolically their ideas, feelings and perceptions about self and others. Conflicts can be resolved and self esteem is increased while coping skills are developed.

Educational concepts about divorce are presented in six units and should be followed in order. Each child will need a small box of crayons. Crayons are suggested because they are more effective for expressing feelings. Ask children to draw any picture that comes into their mind when they read the words on each page. They may ask for more directions or suggestions but need to be encouraged to make their own decisions and draw their own ideas. Emphasize ideas and expressions rather than drawing ability. When thinking about difficult emotional issues, children often regress and scribble, erase, cross-out or draw something unrelated.

It is important to have a supportive and well prepared adult to acknowledge and accept feelings and encourage communication. Books from the adult reading list should be read before beginning. Supplemental reading for children is suggested also. A facilitator guide is available from the publisher for group use.

This book was designed to teach children some concepts about divorce and to recognize and express feelings of grief from family change, to encourage open communication and to help adults discover unhealthy misconceptions children may have. The concepts and following objectives are included in the text and may be stressed by additional reading from the books suggested for children.

I. CHANGE IS PART OF LIFE p.1-4
    See change as a natural part of growth
    Discuss personal change
    Identify ways of coping with change
    Discuss changes related to divorce

II. UNDERSTANDING DIVORCE p.5-9
    Learn concepts of marriage and divorce
    Assess placement of blame
    Identify misconceptions
    Recognize personal changes

III. FEELINGS ABOUT DIVORCE p.10-15
    Recognize grief as a reaction to loss
    Accept all feelings as o.k.
    Recognize/name basic feelings
    Identify difficult feelings

IV. EXPRESSING FEELINGS p. 16-21
    Identify fears and worries
    Recognize unhealthy misconceptions
    Learn healthy ways to express feelings
    Begin sharing feelings

V. LIVING WITH DIVORCED PARENTS p.22-27
    Recognize parent's feelings
    Increase confidence and self esteem
    Learn ways to communicate concerns
    Develop good self care

VI. LIVING WELL IN A CHANGING WORLD p.28-32
    Recognize individual strengths
    Identify support systems
    Strengthen relationships
    Celebrate book completion

TO EACH PARENT:

Divorce is a painful difficult time for adults. It can be even more difficult for children. This book was designed to help your child understand and express the feelings they have about your separation or divorce. It is easier for most children to draw their feelings than to verbalize them. They learn symbols before they learn words. The confusing feelings about divorce can be very stressful for most children. Some children may stuff their feelings and they may turn into headaches, stomach aches or behavior problems.

Both parents should do some of the suggested reading about divorce before children begin work on their books. You will be better prepared and more understanding about their drawings. Each child will decide if they want to share their book with their parents. I hope you will respect that privilege. They don't want to create additional problems. Allow them to share their book and feelings without any negative comments from you. All feelings are o.k. and will change.

What a child thinks is as powerful as what actually happened. Be gentle if you see misconceptions and correct them gently at another time. Remember that a child identifies with both parents. If one parent is seen as very bad they are likely to see themselves as bad also. Listen to their pictures and find ways to help them learn to cope with change and loss and continue loving and trusting important role models.

SUGGESTED READING FOR ADULTS

Clarke, Jeanne, SELF ESTEEM: A FAMILY AFFAIR, Minneapolis, MN, Winston Books, 1978

Grollman, Earl, EXPLAINING DIVORCE TO CHILDREN, Boston, Beacon Press, 1989

Lansky, Vicki, DIVORCE BOOK FOR PARENTS, New York, American Library, 1989

Wallerstein, Judith, SECOND CHANCES, New York, Ticknor & Fields, 1989

Goldstein, Sonja, DIVORCE AND YOUR CHILD, New Haven, Conn. Yale University Press, 1984

ADDITIONAL READING FOR CHILDREN

Alika, (Brandenberg), FEELINGS, New York, Mulberry Books, 1986

Brown, Laurene & Marc, DINOSAURS DIVORCE, Boston, Little Brown & Co., 1986

Boegehold, Betty, DADDY DOESN'T LIVE HERE ANYMORE, New York, Golden Books, Webster Pub. 1985

Gardner, Richard, THE BOYS AND GIRLS BOOK ABOUT DIVORCE, New York, Jason Aronson, 1970

Grollman, Earl, TALKING ABOUT DIVORCE AND SEPARATION: A DIALOGUE BETWEEN PARENT & CHILD, Boston, Beacon Press, 1975

LeShan, Eda, WHATS GOING TO HAPPEN TO ME?, New York, Macmillan Pub., 1978

Rofes, E., THE KIDS' BOOK OF DIVORCE, Lexington, MA., Lewis Pub., 1981

Schuchman, Joan, TWO PLACES TO SLEEP, Minneapolis, CarolRhoda Books, 1979

ADDITIONAL ACTIVITIES

Hammond, J.M., GROUP COUNSELING FOR CHILDREN OF DIVORCE, © Granbrook Publishing Co.
J815 Cranbrook, Ann Arbor, MI 48104

FOR CHILDREN:

This is your book! You will make it special as you draw the pictures that come into your mind as you read the words on each page. There will never be another book just like yours.

This book was written to help you understand the many feelings children have about divorce. There are many changes when parents decide they cannot live together and must separate or divorce. It is often a difficult time for everyone.

You do not have to be able to draw or color well to add your thoughts and feelings to this book. You will need just a small box of crayons to draw lines shapes and perhaps a few words to tell some things you think or feel about the changes in your life. There is no right or wrong way. Do it your way.

Begin with the first page and do the pages in order. Don't skip pages. When you have one or a few pages, stop and share your work with an adult who cares about you. You will discover that you feel better after you have talked about your feelings with someone. You may decide you want to share your book with each of your parents so they can learn about your feelings too.

Change is part of life. Living → Growing → Changing
Change in nature is easy to see. →

→   → → Draw more...

People change too.

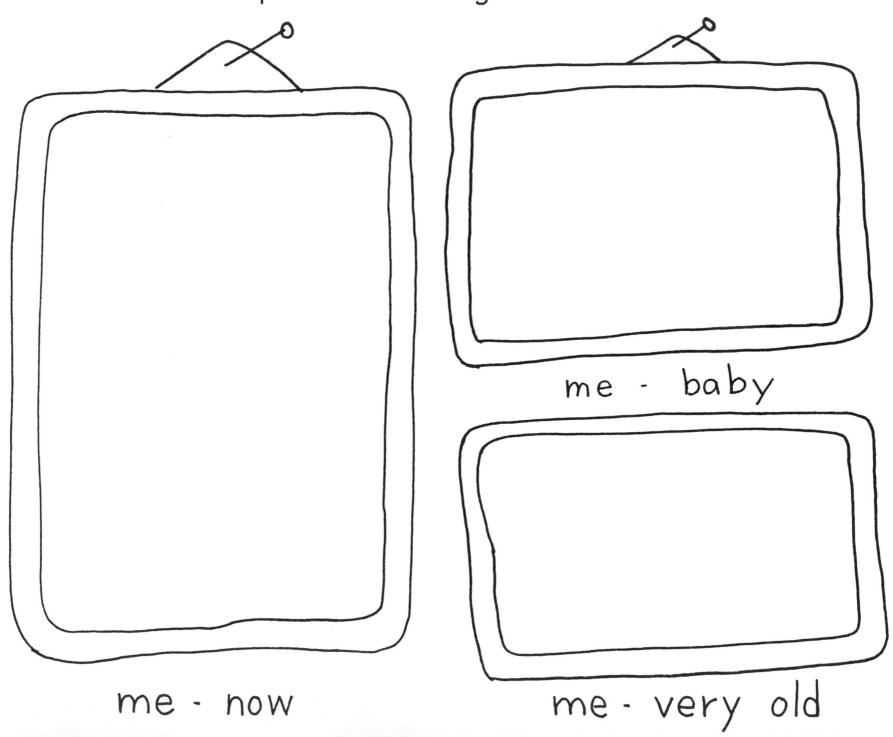

me - baby

me - now

me - very old

2.

Families change when people die or get born, move in or out, get married or divorced. My family has changed because... (draw a picture about this)

3.

There may be many changes when parents separate. One parent has to find a new place to live. There may be less money. Children may not see one parent as often.

It may all be hard to understand. Children may
4. wonder why their parents don't love each other.

Marriage

After drawing a picture of marriage, write some reasons you think people get married.

Marriage is a legal promise two people make. They plan to live together forever, but sometimes they discover they have a great <u>many</u> problems!

1. Anger builds and they fight about many things.
2. They may say or do terrible things.
3. They lose trust, love and interest.
4. They stop talking and solving problems.
5. They try but are unable to change.
6. They don't like to be together.

7. They may find someone else to love.
8. They decide their marriage was a big mistake.
9. They decide to separate and one moves out.
10. They have many feelings!

Divorce

After you draw a picture of divorce, write some reasons you think people get divorced.

Divorce is the legal ending of a marriage. Parents divorce each other, but they do not divorce their children. Parents will continue to love their children and take care of them even though they do not live together.

1. There will be many changes.
2. It will be a difficult time for all.
3. Parents may be busier, angry and sad.
4. Divorce is final. Most people do not get back together.
5. Children may have two places to live.
6. Most children will still love both parents
7. Children will have many feelings.

Children's lives change when parents separate. Something important may be lost. What have you lost that was important to you?

Divorce may bring many <u>feelings</u> about change. The pain from loss and change is called <u>GRIEF</u>.

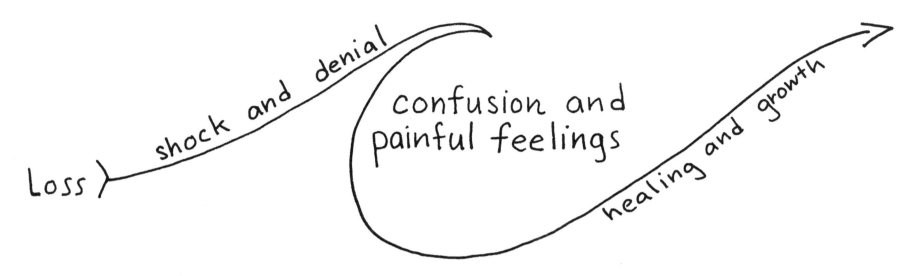

Loss
shock and denial
confusion and painful feelings
healing and growth

Grief comes and goes like waves in the ocean. There will be stormy times ... There will be calm times.

Feelings are all O.K. Feelings change. (draw some feeling faces)

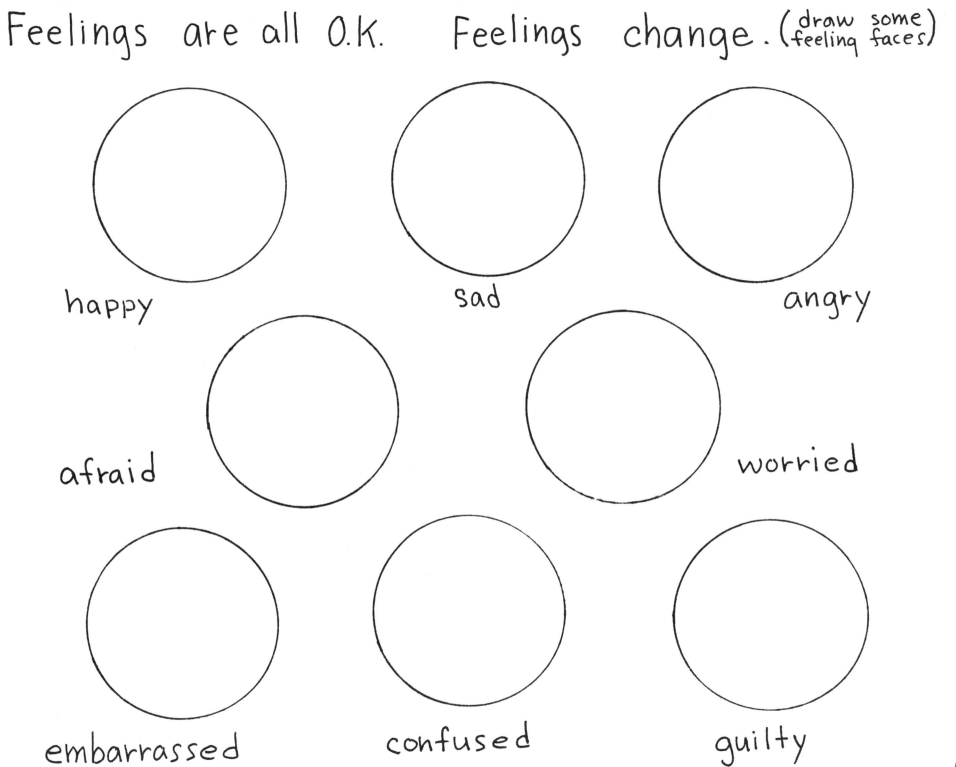

happy

sad

angry

afraid

worried

embarrassed

confused

guilty

11.

Sometimes people put on a "mask" to hide feelings they don't want to show. (name and draw 3 feelings you sometimes hide from others)

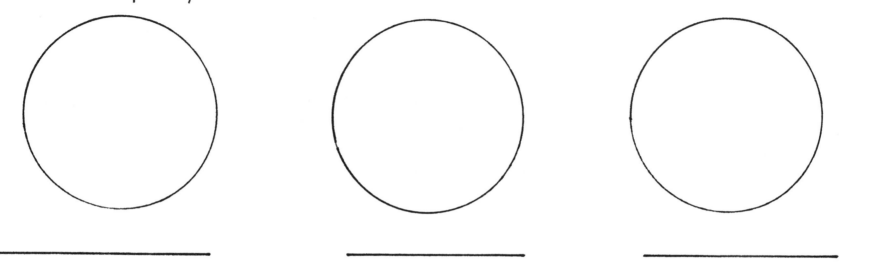

Name and draw the "mask" you might hide the feeling with.

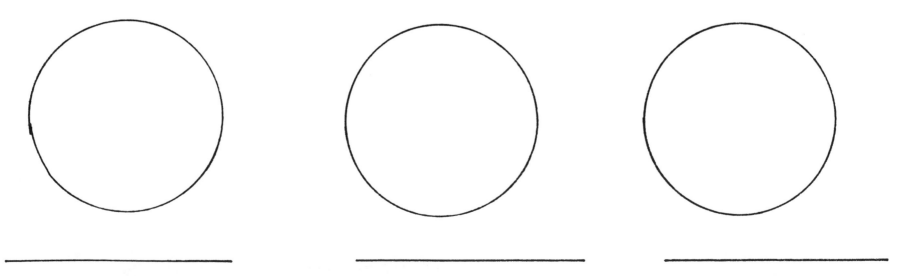

Feelings are something you <u>feel in your body.</u>

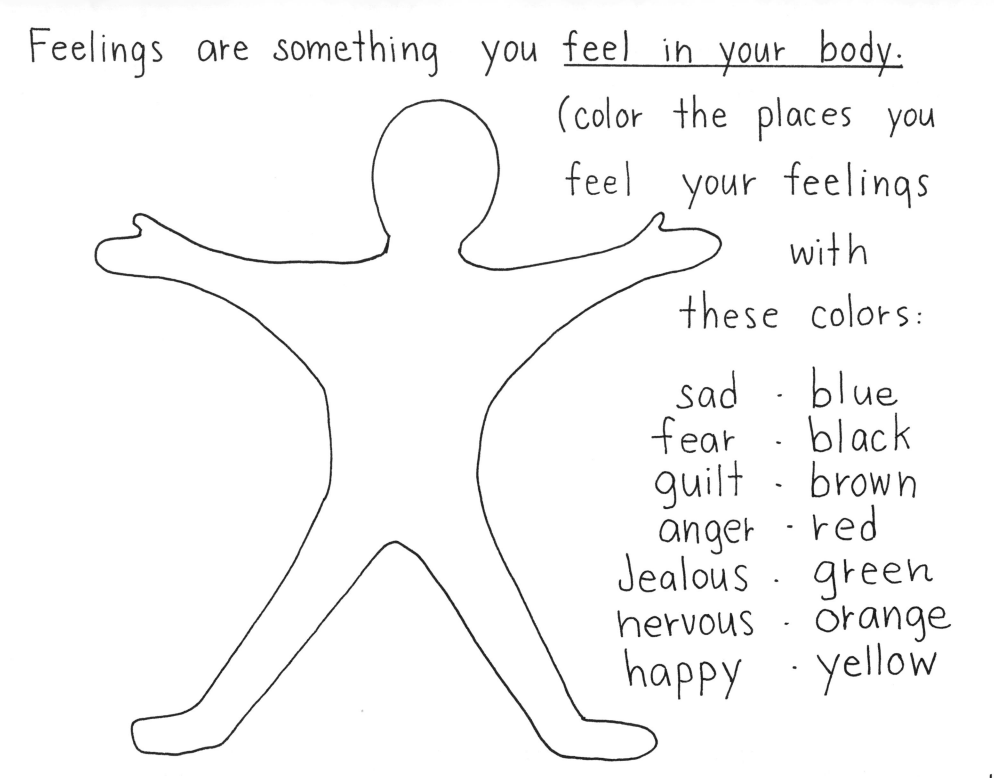

(color the places you feel your feelings with these colors:

sad · blue
fear · black
guilt · brown
anger · red
Jealous · green
nervous · orange
happy · yellow

If feelings are stuffed inside too long they may cause aches and pains.

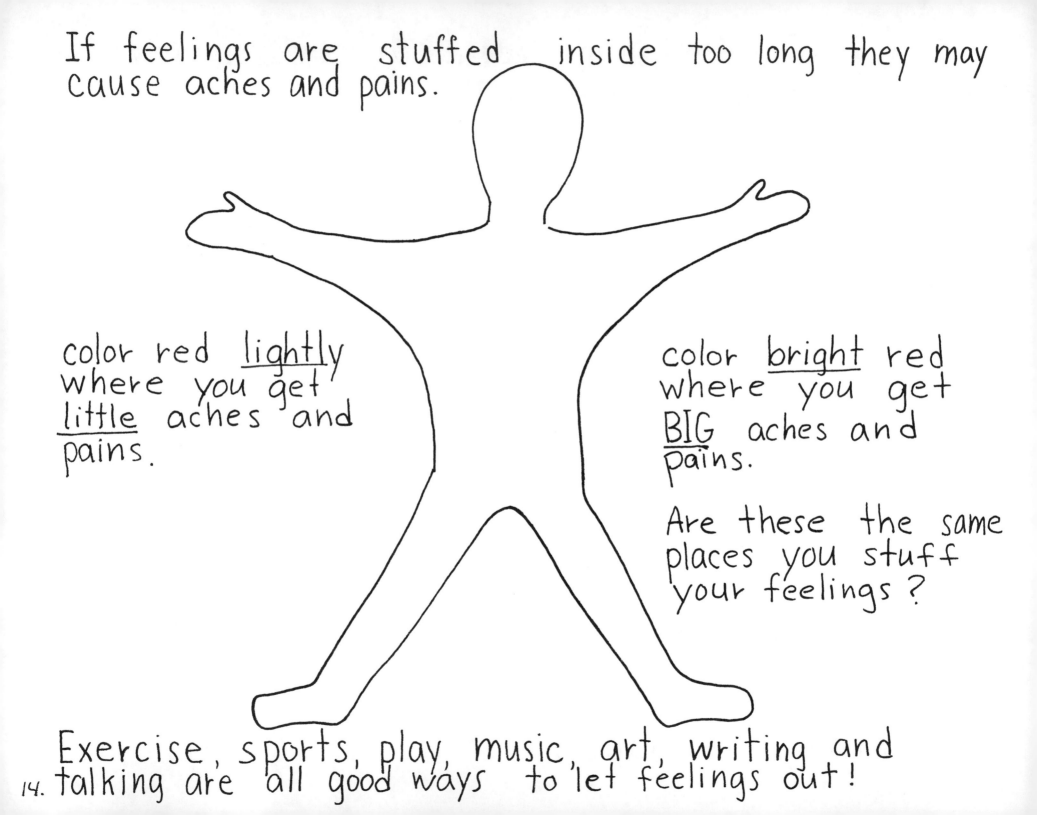

color red <u>lightly</u> where you get <u>little</u> aches and pains.

color <u>bright</u> red where you get <u>BIG</u> aches and pains.

Are these the same places you stuff your feelings?

Exercise, sports, play, music, art, writing and talking are all good ways to let feelings out!

14.

Check the feelings you feel <u>sometimes</u> with <u>✓</u> or
<u>✓✓✓</u> if <u>often.</u> (underline any words you don't understand)

scared	nervous	smart
brave	sad	empty
lonely	unloved	disgusted
confused	ignored	jealous
proud	angry	shamed
loved	afraid	embarrassed
cheated	excited	frustrated
miserable	bored	disappointed
furious	special	guilty
stupid	happy	worried

15.

Everyone feels angry at times. I get angry when...

When I feel angry, I...

It is O.K. to feel angry, but it is <u>not</u> O.K. to
hurt <u>people</u> or <u>things</u>! (circle things you do that
are <u>O.K.</u> and put a big "X" over things that are
<u>not</u> <u>O.K.</u> to do when you are angry.)   17.

You can <u>learn</u> to let anger out in ways that <u>will</u> <u>not</u> <u>hurt</u> <u>people</u> or <u>things</u>. O.K. ways are:

1. Saying "I am angry because... "

2. Punching a pillow or punching ball.

3. Yelling into a pillow or in the shower.

4. Stomping you feet or clapping your hands.

5. Write an angry letter and tear it up.

6. Writing in your journal.

7. Scribble on an old newspaper using alot of color and feeling. Scrunch it into a ball to toss at a blank wall.

8. Walk or run fast.

18. You are responsible for your <u>behavior</u>!

Children __may__ feel VERY sad about divorce.

It's O.K. to cry! Crying let's the sadness out and helps people feel better.

When parents separate, there may be times when their children feel frightened.

20. Drawing something scary makes it less frightening.

Divorce may also bring some good changes.

Before   After

Parents have many feelings about divorce too!
What do <u>you</u> think <u>your</u> parents are feeling?

Mom   Dad

Children can't fix parent's problems. Children
22. can't <u>start</u> or <u>stop</u> divorce.   Divorce is a grown-up problem!

Parents may not like each other after they divorce. They may still fight about things.

But... it is still O.k. for children to love <u>both</u> parents. 23.

Everyone has something they wonder or worry about. Children have the right to ask questions. Parents have the right to answer or not.

I'd like to ask Mom...   I'd like to ask Dad...

Children can say "NO"! They don't have to listen to bad things about either parent.

And... they don't have to be message carriers!

Children may need to help and do more for themselves, but they can't be Moms or Dads. They can't take the place of either parent. Children need to be children.

There are things I like about me...

My parents don't live together but they <u>both</u> love me!

27.

There are some things I am good at...

Everyone is good at something. No one is
28. good at everything.

There are things I like to do with Mom.

We will have many good times together. 29.

There are things I like to do with Dad.

30. We will have many good times together.

There will be many good times. Many people care about me and I will <u>always</u> be taken care of.
(list names... and place number in "caring circle")

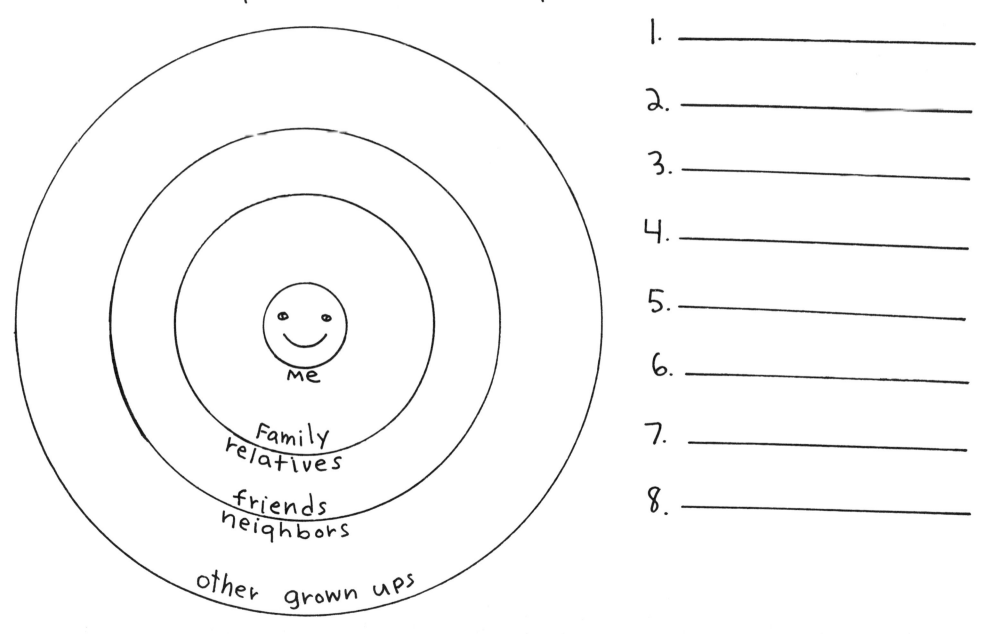

1. _____
2. _____
3. _____
4. _____
5. _____
6. _____
7. _____
8. _____

31.

I can wish for some happy changes in my life.!

32. Life keeps changing. I am learning to cope with change and all kinds of feelings. I am O.K. !

The Drawing Out Feelings Series

This new series designed by Marge Heegaard provides parents and professionals with an organized approach to helping children ages 6-12 cope with feelings resulting from family loss and change.

Designed to be used in an adult/child setting, these workbooks provide age-appropriate educational concepts and questions to help children identify and accept their feelings. Children are given the opportunity to work out their emotions during difficult times while learning to recognize acceptable behavior, and conflicts can be resolved and self-esteem increased while the coping skills for loss and change are being developed.

All four titles are formatted so that children can easily illustrate their answers to the important questions in the text.

When Something Terrible Happens

A workbook to help children deal with their feelings about traumatic events.

Empowers children to explore feelings, and reduces nightmares and post-traumatic stress symptoms. "This healing book...combines story, pictures, information, and art therapy in a way that appeals to children." —Stephanie Frogge, Director of Victim Outreach, M.A.D.D.

Ages 6-12, 36 pp, 11x8 1/2", $6.95
trade paperback, ISBN 0-9620502-3-7

When Mom and Dad Separate

A workbook to help children deal with their feelings about separation/divorce.

This bestselling workbook helps youngsters discuss the basic concepts of marriage and divorce, allowing them to work through all the powerful and confusing feelings resulting from their parents' decision to separate.

Ages 6-12, 36 pp, 11x8 1/2", $6.95
trade paperback, ISBN 0-9620502-2-9

When Someone Has a Very Serious Illness

A workbook to help children deal with their feelings about serious illness.

An excellent resource for helping children learn the basic concepts of illness and various age-appropriate ways of coping with someone else's illness. "...offers children a positive tool for coping with those many changes." —Christine Ternand, M.D., Pediatrician

Ages 6-12, 41 pp, 11 x 8 1/2", $6.95
trade paperback, ISBN 0-9620502-4-5

When Someone Very Special Dies
Children Can Learn to Cope with Grief

A workbook to help children deal with their feelings about death.

Here is a practical format for allowing children to understand the concept of death and develop coping skills for life. Children, with adult supervision, are invited to illustrate and personalize their loss through art. This workbook encourages the child to identify support systems and personal strengths. "I especially appreciate the design of this book...the child becomes an active participant in pictorially and verbally doing something about [their loss]." —Dean J. Hempel, M.D., Child Psychiatrist

Ages 6–12
36 pp, 11 x 8 1/2", $6.95
trade paperback
ISBN 0-9620502-0-2

When a Family Is In Trouble
Children Can Cope With Grief From Drug and Alcohol Addictions

A workbook to help children through the trauma of a parent's chemical dependency problem.

This helpful workbook provides basic information about addictions and encourages healthy coping skills. Children express personal trauma and feelings more easily in pictures than in words, and the pages of this title are perfect to "draw out" those feelings and hurts. There is plenty of room for a child's artwork.

Ages 6-12
36 pp, 11 x 8 1/2", $6.95
trade paperback
ISBN 0-9620502-7-X

When a Parent Marries Again

A workbook to help children deal with their feelings about stepfamilies.

This book helps kids sort through unrealistic expectations, different values, divided loyalties, and family histories. It helps reduce the fear and stress surrounding remarriage and promotes greater family unity.

Ages 6-12, 36 pp, 11 x 8 1/2", $6.95
trade paperback, ISBN 0-9620502-6-1

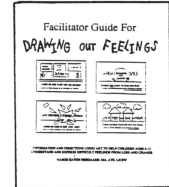

Facilitator Guide For DRAWING OUT FEELINGS

for
When Someone Very Special Dies
When Something Terrible Happens
When Someone Has a Very Serious Illness
When Mom and Dad Separate

Structure and suggestions for helping children, individually or in groups, cope with feelings from family change. Includes directions for six organized sessions for each of the four workbooks.
99 pp. 8½x11 ISBN 0-9620502-5-3
$20.00

SEND THIS INFORMATION TO ORDER

SHIPPING CHARGES
up to 19.99 $2.50 * 20.00-44.99 $3.50 * 45.00-74.99 $4.50 * over 75.00 $5.50

Grades 3-6
64 pages $15.95

Stories about young people's grief and facts about death.

Coping with Death & Grief

___ Copies COPING WITH DEATH AND GRIEF ($15.95)
___ Copies DRAWING OUT FEELINGS GUIDE ($20.00)
___ Copies WHEN SOMEONE VERY SPECIAL DIES *
___ Copies WHEN SOMEONE HAS A VERY SERIOUS ILLNESS *
___ Copies WHEN SOMETHING TERRIBLE HAPPENS *
___ Copies WHEN MOM AND DAD SEPARATE *
___ Copies WHEN A PARENT MARRIES AGAIN *
___ Copies WHEN A FAMILY IS IN TROUBLE *

* at the following prices: *quantity discounts*

order amount	each cost	shipping
1-11	$ 6.95	$ 2.50
12-24	$ 4.50	$ 4.25
25-79	$ 4.00	$ 7.25
80-(same)	$ 3.50	$10.50

FOR FOREIGN ORDERS: PAYMENT IN USA FUNDS ONLY.
DOUBLE SHIPPING CHARGES.
Make check payable and send to:
WOODLAND PRESS
99 Woodland Circle
Minneapolis, MN. 55424
(612) 926-2665

Total order _____
MN. res. 6.5% _____
Handling _____
TOTAL COST _____

NAME _____

ORGANIZATION _____

ADDRESS _____

_____

_____

TELEPHONE (____) _____